Introduction

1 Quick meals 5

2 Main Meals 19

3 Side Dishes 37

Salad dressings and sauces 44

Marinades 45

Weights and measures 46

Index 48

contents

Barbecue

Barbecue cooking is part of the modern way of life. Long before the new barbeques were introduced, people were slapping on steaks and sausages on many a makeshift barbie in the backyard and the forests. Two rows of bricks and an iron grill placed across the top was the usual self fashioned backyard barbie.

The backyard barbies are still with us, upgraded to appliances of various degrees of performance and sophistication, and elevated in status from the 'backyard' to the pool area, terrace, patio, balcony and even a special garden barbecue area.

All types of barbecues will produce delicious foods, and barbecue cooking is a relaxing way of cooking which is also fun. Family and friends gather around to socialise and cook at the same time. The purpose of this book is to help you get the best from your barbecue experience.

The book is divided into sections according to cooking times.

The 'Quick Meals' section will give you many ideas for barbie parties, foods which can be produced quickly for a crowd with maximum flavour. The 'Main Meals and 'Side Dishes' will help you produce outdoor family meals and with entertaining a few friends.

So light up the barbie, throw on the steaks, slap on the marinade and enjoy.

introduction

Cooking Methods for Barbecues

Direct Heat Method – This is the traditional barbecue method where food is cooked directly over the heat source on the grill bars or hot plate. It sears the meat, seals in the juices and produces a characteristic chargrilled appearance. Fatty meats may cause flare-ups on charcoal and gas barbecues if cooked on the grill bars. If this occurs, move meat to the hot plate after searing on both sides or place a sheet of heavy duty foil under the meat, if a hot plate is not available. Direct heat is suitable for thinner foods which will cook quickly.

Pre-heat the grill with flame or burners on high. When flame settles down or gas heat has reached a constant temperature, adjust the burners to the temperature noted in the recipe.

Indirect Heat Method – The heat source is indirect, that is the food is placed on the grill bars with the heat coming from the sides, under the bars instead of directly under. It is a slower method of cooking than direct heat and is suitable for thicker cuts to large roasts and whole chickens. A drip tray is placed in the centre between the heat source to catch the drips. Fatty meats are best cooked over indirect heat a there are no dangerous flare-ups.

Pre-heat the grill with flame or burners on high. When flame settles down or gas heat has reached a constant temperature, turn-off the centre burners and adjust the side burners to the temperature noted in the recipe. If using a charcoal barbeque, arrange hot coals evenly on each side of the charcoal grate. Place food in the centre of the cooking grate. A drip pan is useful to collect drippings that can be used for gravies and sauces, it will also prevent flare-ups.

Handy barbecue tools

Don't forget that barbecues get hot, so it is important to have the necessary tools and equipment ready before you begin. Set up a table near the barbecue to lay out the necessary items.

Items of Most Importance for Safety

• Long tongs to move glowing coals or to reach across the hotplate or hot grill to turn foods.

• Long handled flat lifter to lift and turn hamburgers, egg and fish.

• A turning spatula, side and strong to turn hamburgers and flatten them as they cook.

• Insulated gloves for adjusting hot racks, hot vents or anything else too hot to touch.

• Long handled basting brush.

• Fish grill or fish cage to make turning whole fish safer and easier.

• A bucket of water on stand by for any emergency.

quick meals

teriyaki prawns (shrimp)

1kg/35oz fresh green
prawns (shrimp) in shell,
normal or king

teriyaki marinade
(page 45)

bamboo skewers, soaked

1 Shell the prawns (shrimp), leaving the tails intact. Place in a non-metal dish and smother with the marinade. Cover and refrigerate for 1 or 2 hours. Thread onto soaked skewers. For small prawns (shrimp) thread 2 or 3 per skewer; for king prawns (shrimp) thread only one from tail-end to top.

2 Heat the barbecue and place a square of baking paper on the grill bars. Place the prawns (shrimp) on the grill brushing with marinade on both sides as they cook. Cook until prawns (shrimp) turn pink in colour. Take care not to overcook.

Yield 10

hot dogs with mustard relish

1kg/35oz frankfurters or thin sausages

225mL/8oz barbecue sauce

12 hot dog rolls
mild mustard for serving

gherkin relish or tomato pickles to serve

1 Heat the barbecue and oil the grill bars. Place frankfurters or sausages, turn to heat on the grill evenly, so the skin does not burst. Continue to cook for 10-12 minutes, brushing with a little barbecue sauce as they are turned. Push to cooler part of barbecue if cooking too quickly or turn down the heat.

2 Split the rolls, keeping the 2 halves attached and place cutside down on hot plate to toast.

3 Fill the roll with frankfurter or sausage, squeeze a row of mustard along the side and spoon in the gherkin relish or tomato pickle.

shish kebabs

750g/35oz lamb neck fillet, cut into 2½cm/1in pieces

fresh mint to garnish and lemon wedges to serve

For the marinade

100g/3½oz Greek yoghurt

½ small onion, grated

2 cloves garlic, crushed

juice of ½ lemon

1 tbsp olive oil

3 tbsp chopped fresh mint

salt and black pepper

1 To make the marinade, mix together the yoghurt, onion, garlic, lemon juice, oil, mint and seasoning in a large non-metallic bowl. Add the lamb and stir to coat. Cover with cling film and refrigerate for 4 hours or overnight.

2 Preheat the grill to high. Thread the lamb onto 4 or 8 metal skewers, depending on their size. Grill the kebabs for 10-12 minutes, turning the skewers 2-3 times, until cooked through. Garnish with mint and serve with lemon wedges.

Note: If you've ever been to Greece, these tender kebabs will bring memories flooding back. Serve them with rice, a large Greek salad and some tzatziki on the side.

perfect

T-Bone steak

4 T-bone steaks

2 tsps crushed garlic

2 tsps oil

salt and pepper

Garlic Butter

55g/2oz butter

1 tsp crushed garlic

1 tbsp parsley flakes

2 tsps lemon juice

mix all ingredients together and serve in a pot with a spoon

1 Bring the steaks to room temperate. Mix garlic, oil and salt and pepper together. Rub onto both sides of the steak. Stand for 10-15 minutes at room temperature.

2 Heat the barbecue until hot and oil the grill bars. Arrange the steaks and sear for one minute each side. Move steaks to cooler part of the barbecue to continue cooking over moderate heat, or turn heat down. If heat cannot be reduced then elevate on a wire cakerack placed on the grill bars. Cook until desired doneness is achieved. Total time 5/6 minutes for rare, 7-10 minutes for medium and 10-14 minutes for well done. Turn during cooking.

3 Serve on a heated steak plate and top with a dollop of garlic butter. Serve with potatoes.

Serves 4

Note: Many a time this delicious steak has been ruined on the barbecue. Cook on all barbecues and improvise a hood if using a flattop barbecue.

toasted

steak sandwiches

510g/18oz topside steak

2 tbsps lemon juice

1 tsp crushed garlic

salt and pepper

1 tbsp oil

butter for spreading

10 slices toasted bread

2 large onions, thinly sliced

1 tbsp oil

steak sauce of choice

1 Cut the topside steak into 4 or 5 pieces and pound with a meat mallet until thin. Place in a non-metal container. Mix the lemon juice, garlic, salt, pepper and oil together and pour over the steaks. Turn to coat both sides and marinate for 30 minutes at room temperature, or longer in the refrigerator.

2 Soften the butter and spread a thin coating on both sides of the bread. If desired mix a little garlic into the butter.

3 Heat barbecue until hot and oil the grill bars and hotplate. Place onions on the hotplate. Toss and drizzle with a little oil as they cook. When beginning to soften, push to one side and turn occasionally with tongs. Place toast on hotplate and cook until golden on both sides. Place steaks on grill bars and cook 2 minutes on each side.

4 Assemble sandwiches as food cooks by placing steak and onions on one slice of toast, topping with a good squirt of steak sauce and closing with second slice of toast.

Yields 5 sandwiches

Patties

510g/18oz ground
chicken meat

$1/2$ tsp salt

$1/4$ tsp pepper

1 tsp crushed garlic

$1/2$ tsp fresh chopped
chilli or chilli powder

2 tbsps dried
breadcrumbs

55mL/2fl oz water

Flapjacks

145g/5oz plain flour

$1/4$ tsp baking powder

$1/4$ tsp salt

2 tbsps chopped basil

1 tsp crushed garlic

170mL/6fl oz milk

1 egg

Chilli yoghurt sauce

200g/7oz natural yoghurt

2 tsps sweet chilli sauce
or to taste

mix well together

1 Mix all patty ingredients together and knead a little with one hand to distribute ingredients and make it fine in texture. Cover and rest in refrigerator for 20 minutes. With wet hands, form into small flat patties about $2^1/2$cm/1in in diameter. Place on a flat tray until needed and refrigerate.

2 Prepare batter for flapjacks. Sift the flour, baking powder and salt into a bowl.
Mix together the blended basil and garlic and the milk, then beat in the egg. Make a well in the centre of the flour and pour in the milk mixture. Stir to form a smooth batter. Cover and set aside for 20 minutes.

3 Heat barbecue until hot and oil the grill bars and hotplate. Brush the patties with a little oil and place on grill bars. Grill for 2 minutes each side, cook the flapjacks at the same time, pour 55mL/2fl oz of mixture onto the greased hotplate. Cook until bubbles appear over the surface and the bottom is golden. Flip over with an eggslice and cook until golden. Transfer to a clean towel and cover to keep hot.

4 Serve a flapjack on each plate and arrange 3 patties on top with a dollop of chilli yoghurt sauce.

5 Serve with a side salad and the extra flapjacks.
Serves 6

2kg/70oz chicken wings, tips removed

1 quantity soy and honey marinade (page 45)

3 tbsps sesame seeds, toasted

quick sesame chicken wings

1 Place wings in a large container and smother with the marinade. Cover and marinade for 30 minutes at room temperature or longer in the refrigerator.

2 Place half the wings in a microwave-safe dish and microwave for 10 minutes on high. Remove and microwave the remainder.

3 Heat the barbecue until hot. Place a wire cake-rack over the grill bars and place the wings on the rack. Brush with marinade left in the bow. Turn and brush the wings frequently until they are brown and crisp.

4 Spread sesame seeds on a foil tray and place on the barbecue. Shake occasionally as they toast. Sprinkle over the browned chicken wings.

Serve as finger food.

Yields 24 wings

quick

sausage sizzle

2kg/70oz pork or beef
sausages

1kg/70oz onions, thinly
sliced

honey & chilli marinade
(page 45)

1 Place sausages in a large saucepan and cover with cold water. Heat slowly until simmering point is reached, then simmer for 5 minutes. Drain well. If not required immediately refrigerate until needed.

2 Heat the barbecue until hot and grease grill bars with oil. Pour the honey and chilli marinade into a heatproof bowl and place at the side of the barbecue. Arrange sausages from left to right on the grill bars or hotplate and brush with the marinade. Turn and brush with marinade after one minute and continue turning and basting for 10 minutes until sausages are well glazed and cook through. Give a final brushing with marinade as they are removed to a serving platter.

3 To cook onions, oil the hot plate and place on the onion slices. Toss at intervals, drizzle with a little oil as they cook. Serve the honey and glazed sausages with the onions and accompany with salad and garlic bread.

Note: This method is suitable for cooking a large number of sausages to serve around. Pork or beef thick sausages are used, which are simmered in water before placing on the barbecue. This prevents the thick sausages from splitting and reduces the cooking time on the barbecue. Calculate the amount of sausages needed for the number of people to be served.

honey chicken drumsticks

2kg/70oz chicken drumsticks (medium-size)

370mL/13 oz honey and chilli marinade (page 45)

Mustard Cream Sauce

300mL/10½oz carton sour cream

250g Dijon mustard

115mL/4oz honey and chilli marinade (page 45)

I Place drumsticks in a non-metal container and pour enough marinade over to coat well. Cover and stand 30 minutes at room temperature or longer in the refrigerator.

2 To cook, prepare barbecue as follows:

Kettle and Hooded Barbecues – Heat until hot, place drumsticks over indirect heat and cover with lid or hood. Cook for 15 minutes. Remove hood, turn drumsticks and brush with marinade every 8 minutes, replacing hood until cooked approximately 45 minutes cooking time. Continue turning and brushing with marinade as above 3 more times at 8 minute intervals or until drumsticks are cooked through to the bone. Total cooking time 40-45 minutes.

Flat-top, Charcoal and Gas Barbecues –Heat the barbecue until hot. Place a wire cake-rack over the grill bars and oil the rack. The rack should stand 2½cm/1in above the bars. Place the drumsticks on the rack and cook for 15-20 minutes, turning frequently. Place a square of baking paper onto the grill bars. Transfer the drumsticks onto the baking paper. Brush with marinade and turn frequently. Cook for a further 10-15 minutes until well glazed and cooked to the bone.

Mustard Cream Sauce: Mix the sour cream, mustard, honey & chilli marinade together in a heat-proof bowl. Place at the side of the barbecue to heat through. Serve drumsticks with the mustard cream sauce and vegetable accompaniments or salad.

barbecued

Bread

plain focaccia

Turkish bread

mini dampers

bread rolls

firm bread loaf, sliced

Butters

butter or margarine

tandoori paste (page 45)

Thai flavour base

pesto

I Mix one part butter or margarine with a part flavouring to taste. Lightly spread both sides of sliced bread or rolls with flavoured butter of your choice. Place on heated hot plate and cook until golden on both sides.

2

main
meals

piquant pork fillets with polenta

4 pork fillets 300g/10½oz each
170g/6oz jar sun-dried tomato pesto
1 tbsp chopped basil
2 tbsps lemon juice
1 tbsp olive oil
1 quantity polenta

1 To make marinade: mix together sun-dried tomato pesto, chopped basil, lemon juice and olive oil.

2 Carefully remove the silvery white membrane from the top of the fillets with a sharp pointed knife. Place fillets in a suitable container and cover both sides with half of the marinade, (reserving remainder). Cover and marinate for 30 minutes at room temperature, or longer in the refrigerator.

3 Cook as follows: <u>Charcoal Kettle or Hooded Gas Barbecue</u> - Prepare barbecue for indirect cooking. Place the fillets on oiled grill bars over the drip tray. Cook with lid on for 40 minutes. Brush twice with some of the remaining capsicum mixture used for marinade. When fillets are almost cooked, cut prepared polenta into 10x7cm/4x3in slabs, remove from dish and brush with oil. Place over direct heat and cook for 4 minutes on each side until golden.

<u>Flat-top and Electric Barbecue Grills</u> - Heat until hot. Place a wire cake-rack to stand 2½cm/1in above grill bars. Place fillets on cake-rack and cook for approximately 20 minutes each side. Brushing with marinade when turned. Cut polenta as above and cook on oiled grill bars 5 minutes on each side.

To serve: Slice the fillets into 2½cm/1in thick diagonal slices. Overlap onto the polenta slice and top with the reserved and warmed tomato mixture.

Serve with suitable vegetables.

Serves 4–6

glazed

1kg/35oz pork spare ribs
(American-Style)

soy and honey marinade
(page 45)

1 Place spare ribs on a large sheet of heavy-duty foil and cover both sides generously with marinade. Wrap into a double-folded parcel, making sure all joins are well-sealed to prevent leakage. Stand for at least half an hour before cooking. Place in refrigerator if not to be cooked immediately.

2 Prepare the barbecue for direct-heat cooking. Place a wire cake-rack on the grill bars to stand 2½cm/1 in above the bars. Place ribs in the foil parcel on the rack and cook for 10 minutes each side.

3 Remove to a plate, remove ribs and discard foil, then return ribs to rack. Continue cooking brushing with fresh sauce or marinade and turning each minute until ribs are well browned and crisp (about 10 minutes). Total cooking time is approximately 30-35 minutes.

Note: Ribs may be cooked by indirect heat in a hooded barbecue. There is no need to wrap in foil. Place over indirect heat after marinating. Brush and turn frequently with lid down for 1 hour or more. Cooking in the foil over direct heat cuts cooking time in half. May be cooked on all barbecues using direct heat.

Serves 4

chicken with mango salsa

4 skinless boneless chicken breasts

1 tbsp olive oil

2 tbsp Thai fish sauce

juice of 1/2 lime

salt and black pepper

fresh mint to garnish and lime wedges to serve

For the salsa

1/2 red pepper (capsicum), deseeded and quartered

1 mango

1 small red chilli, deseeded and finely chopped

1 tbsp olive oil

juice of 1/2 lime

1 tbsp each chopped fresh coriander (cilantro) and mint

1 Place the chicken breasts between cling film and pound with a rolling pin to flatten them slightly. Unwrap and place in a non-metallic dish. Combine the oil, fish sauce, lime juice and seasoning and pour over the chicken. Cover and leave to marinate in the fridge for 1 hour.

2 Meanwhile, make the salsa. Preheat the grill to high. Grill the pepper (capsicum) for 10 minutes, cool, then peel off the skin and dice. Peel the mango, cut the flesh away from the stone and chop. Combine the chopped mango, pepper, chilli, oil, lime juice and herbs in a bowl and season. Cover and refrigerate.

3 Heat a ridged cast-iron grill pan over a medium to high heat. Wipe with the marinade, using a folded piece of kitchen towel. Alternatively, heat 1 teaspoon of the marinade in a heavy-based frying pan. Add the chicken and fry for 3-5 minutes on each side, until cooked through (you may have to do this in batches). Serve with the salsa, garnished with mint and lime.

Serves 4

swordfish steaks

115g/4oz unsalted butter
2 tbsps finely chopped coriander (cilantro)
1 tbsp grated parmesan cheese
4 swordfish steaks
1 tbsp olive oil
4 zucchinis (courgettes), cut into long slices
1 red capsicum (pepper), quartered

1 Cream the butter until soft and mix in the coriander (cilantro) and parmesan. Pile into butter pot and set aside.

2 Heat barbecue grill until hot and brush with oil. Brush fish steaks with oil, place on grill bars and cook 3-4 minutes each side according to thickness. Brush or spray vegetables with oil and place on grill, cook a few minutes on each side. Remove fish steaks and vegetables to heated plates. Top swordfish steak with a generous dollop of coriander (cilantro) butter mixture and serve immediately.

Serves 4

capsicum

barbecued whole snapper

1 Cut and scale the fish and rinse well. Pat dry with paper towels.

2 Mix the capsicum (peppers), basil, lemon juice and oil together. Spoon some into the cavity and spread the remainder over the fish.

3 Lay the fish on a large sheet of oiled foil and roll up the edges to form an enclosure around the fish, leaving the top of the fish exposed (except for flat-top).

Charcoal Kettle and Hooded Gas Barbecue - Place the fish on the grill bars, indirect heat. Cover with lid or hood and cook for 35-40 minutes or until fish flakes when tested with a fork.

Flat Top Charcoal or Gas Barbecue - Prepare fish as above and cover completely with foil. Place on a wire rack and place the rack on top of the grill bars, elevating so that the fish is 10cm/4in above the source of heat. Cook for 10-12 minutes each side. Turn carefully using a large spatula or place fish in a hinged fish rack and turn when needed.

Electric Barbecue Grill - Prepare as for kettle, elevate on a wire rack place on the grill bars. Set barbecue to medium high. Cover with hood and cook 25-35 minutes.

Gherkin Mayonnaise: Mix mayonnaise and gherkin relish or chopped gerkin together. Serve fish while hot with gherkin mayonnaise and accompany with potato wedges and salad.

1 whole snapper (1 ½kg/53oz)
3 tbsps of chopped red capsicum (peppers)
2 tsps chopped fresh basil
2 tbsps lemon juice
1 tbsp olive oil

Gherkin Mayonnaise

1 cup/225mL/8oz mayonnaise
85mL/3oz gherkin relish or chopped gherkins

Serves 4

barbecued

leg of lamb in paper

2kg/4lb leg of lamb

2 tsps salt

1 tsp pepper

115mL/4fl oz lemon juice

2 tblspns freshy crushed garlic

Romano or Parmesan cheese cut into 8x¹/₂cm/ ¹/₅in cubes

170g/6oz jar sun-dried tomato pesto

2 sheets greaseproof paper, oiled

1 sheet brown paper, oiled on both sides

1 Wash the lamb and pat dry. Make about 8 incisions on each side of the lamb with the point of a small knife. Place lamb in a suitable non-corrosive dish, rub all over with salt and pepper and pour over the lemon juice, allowing the juice to enter the incisions. Stand 30 minutes. Push a ¹/₂ teaspoon of crushed garlic into each incision followed by a cheese cube. Rub all over with tomato pesto. Wrap the lamb in the 2 sheets of oiled greaseproof paper and then wrap into a parcel with the brown paper. Tie with kitchen string.

2 Prepare Kettle or Gas Hooded Barbecue for indirect heat on medium-high. Place the lamb parcel onto oiled grill bars over the drip tray and cook, indirect heat, for 2 hours. Turn lamb after 1 hour. When cooked, remove from barbecue and rest for 20 minutes before removing from paper and carving. Take care when opening parcel, that any juices are collected in a bowl. Reheat juices and serve with the carved meat.

3 Serve with a mild mustard, a green salad and garlic bread.   Serves 6–8

lamb

fillets with salsa

2 lamb fillets
about 750g/26ozlb

$^1/_2$ tsp crushed garlic

1 tbsp lemon juice

2 tsps olive oil

salt & pepper

Salsa Pilaf

225g/8oz uncooked rice

6 cups/1$^1/_2$ ltr/53fl oz
boiling water

55g/2oz pine nuts, toasted

300g/10$^1/_2$oz jar
tomato salsa

2 tbsps currants

1 Trim the lamb fillets, removing the fine silver membrane. Place in a dish and add garlic, lemon juice, oil, salt and pepper. Cover and stand 30 minutes. Cook the rice in the boiling, salted water, about 15 minutes, until rice is tender. Drain well and keep hot. Heat a small saucepan, add pine nuts and shake over heat until they colour. Add the salsa and currants and heat through.

2 Heat the barbecue grill plate and oil lightly. Set at medium-high. Place lamb on grill and cook 6-8 minutes, turning to cook on all sides. Cook longer for well done. Rest 5 minutes before slicing in 1cm/$^1/_2$in slices.

3 To Serve: Using a cup or mould, form a mound of rice on the plate. Pour salsa over the rice and arrange lamb slices at base of rice mould.

Serves 4–5

pilaf

garlic

lobster tails with exotic salad

6 green (raw) lobster tails

85g/3oz butter, softened

2 tsps crushed garlic

2 tbsps honey and lemon marinade (page 45)

Exotic Salad

1 avocado, cut into ¹/₂ cm/ ¹/₄ in dice

2 Lebanese cucumbers, diced

¹/₂ small rockmelon, peeled & diced

85mL/3oz honey and lemon marinade (page 45)

1 With kitchen scissors, cut each side of the soft shell on the underside of the lobster tails, and remove. Run a metal skewer through the length of each tail to keep them flat while cooking. Soften the butter and mix in the garlic, and honey and lemon marinade. Spread a coating on the lobster meat.

2 Prepare salad before commencing to cook lobster tails. Mix the diced avocado, cucumber, and rockmelon together. Pour the honey and lemon marinade over the salad. Refrigerate until needed.

3 Heat the barbecue to medium-high and oil the grill bars. Place lobster tails shell-side down and cook until shell turns red. Spread with more butter and turn meat-side down and cook for 5-8 minutes or meat turns white. Turn again and cook 2 minutes more shell-side down. Remove skewers and place on warm plates. Dot with any remaining butter mixture and serve immediately with exotic salad.

Serves 4–6

Mexican

sausages

1kg/35oz thick pork or
beef sausages

2 small packets (55g/2oz)
corn chips, lightly crushed

1 jar tomato salsa

100g/3½oz grated tasty
cheddar cheese

1 Heat barbecue to normal for indirect heat and medium for direct heat, then cook sausages. When cooked, slit each sausage almost through. Open slit and sprinkle in some of the corn chip pieces, spoon in a generous amount of salsa and top with grated cheese. Return to the barbecue grill plate. Prop up so as not to spill filling.

2 Cover with lid or hood and cook until cheese melts, about 1 minute. If using a flat-top or electric barbecue grill, improvise a cover by using a large saucepan lid or overturned baking dish to enclose heat so cheese can melt.

Serves 8

glazed scotch fillet

roast with tomato potato wedges

1½ kg/53oz whole piece of scotch fillet

salt, pepper

2 tsps oil

5 medium-sized potatoes

1 tsp crushed garlic

2 tbsps sun-dried tomato pesto

1 tbsp water

1 tbsp olive oil

herbed wine marinade (page 45)

1 Rub the salt, pepper and oil all over the roast and tie with kitchen string at 2½cm/1in intervals, to keep in shape.

2 Peel and halve the potatoes then cut each half into 4-6 wedges. Rinse potato wedges well, drain and place in a large bowl.

Mix garlic, tomato pesto, water and oil together, pour over wedges and turn to coat well. Place in a large foil dish, in a single layer if possible.

3 Cook as follows:

Kettle and Gas Hooded Barbecue - Prepare charcoal barbecue for normal heat and set gas barbecue to medium-high. Arrange both for indirect cooking. Place the roast over the drip tray, cover with lid or hood and cook for 45 minutes without turning. Proceed to brush with herbed wine marinade every 10 minutes to complete 75 minutes for rare, and 90 minutes for medium. Place potatoes over direct heat for the last 40 minutes of cooking (when you first commence brushing with marinade). Turn wedges over after 20 minutes.

Electric Barbecue Grills - Preheat to medium-high and place a wire cake-rack to stand 2½cm/1in above the grill bars. Place roast in a foil baking dish. Cover with the hood and cook for 40 minutes. Proceed as instructed for kettle and gas barbecues. Place wedges on the hot plate for 40 minutes, turning after 20 minutes.

4 Stand roast covered with foil for 10 minutes before carving. Carve and serve with tomato potato wedges and vegetables or salad of choice.

Serves 8–10

marinated

bolar beef with apple and chilli stuffing

2kg/70oz bolar beef roast

teriyaki marinade (page 45)

Stuffing

1 tbsp butter

1 small onion, thinly sliced

2 rashers bacon, rind removed and chopped

$1/2$ tsps freshly chopped red chilli

1 cooking apple, diced (skin on)

1 Cut a pocket, slanting downwards, in the bolar roast. Place in a suitable non-metal container and smother generously with the marinade. Cover and refrigerate for 24 hours.

2 Prepare the stuffing -Heat butter in a small pan, add onion and bacon and fry for a few minutes, then add the chilli and apple. Stir well and continue to cook for 3 minutes. Allow to cool. Remove the roast from the marinade and pat dry. Place the stuffing in the pocket and close with a skewer or tie roast with kitchen string.

3 Cook as follows: <u>Kettle or Hooded Gas Barbecue</u> - Prepare for indirect heat, medium-high. Place roast on oiled grill bars over the drip tray. Cover with lid or hood and cook for 50 minutes. Lift lid and brush with marinade and continue to brush with marinade every 15 minutes for a total cooking time of $1 1/2$ to 2 hours. Rest the roast, wrapped in foil, for 15 minutes before carving. Carve and serve the roast with vegetables.

<u>Electric Barbecue Grills with Hood</u> - Heat to medium-high. Place a wire cake-rack to stand $2 1/2$cm/1in above grill bars. Place the roast in a foil baking tray and cook as above.

seared

tuna with roasted plum tomatoes

1 clove garlic, finely chopped

finely grated rind and juice of 1 lime

5 tbsp olive oil, plus extra for greasing

3 tbsp chopped fresh rosemary

4 tuna steaks, about 145g/5oz each and 2cm ³/₄in thick

6 plum tomatoes, halved lengthways

1 red onion, halved and thinly sliced lengthways

salt and black pepper

1 Mix together the garlic, lime rind, half the lime juice, 2 tablespoons of the oil and 1 tablespoon of the rosemary in a large dish. Add the tuna and turn to coat evenly. Cover and place in the fridge for 30 minutes to marinate.

2 Preheat the oven to 220°C/425°F/Gas Mark 7. Place the tomatoes and onion in a shallow ovenproof dish with the remaining rosemary. Drizzle with the remaining oil and season. Roast in the oven for 15-20 minutes, until tender and lightly browned.

3 Lightly oil a ridged cast-iron grill pan or large frying pan and heat over a fairly high heat. Add the tuna and cook for 4-5 minutes, turning once, or until golden. Serve with the tomatoes and onion, sprinkled with the remaining lime juice.

Note: Lightly pan-fried tuna is delicious with just a squeeze of lemon or lime juice. But it's the roasted tomatoes, scented with rosemary, that make this dish so hard to beat.

herbed beef salad

2 boneless beef sirloins,
2¹/₂cm/1 in thick

¹/₂ tsp crushed garlic

1 tsp chopped chilli

2 tsps oil

salt, pepper

mixed salad greens
for serving

Herb Dressing

2 tsps basil pesto

1 tsp chopped chilli

1 tbsp chopped parsley

¹/₂ cup/30g/1oz
chopped shallots

15mL/4fl oz olive oil

55mL/2fl oz vinegar

1 Place the steaks in a shallow dish. Mix together the garlic, chilli, oil, salt and pepper and pour over the steaks. Cover and stand 30 minutes.

2 Heat the barbecue grill bars to high and oil the bars. Sear meat 2 minutes on each side then turn down heat a little or move steaks to cooler part of barbecue and cook for 8 minutes on each side. Brush with marinade during cooking. Rest 5 minutes before slicing.

3 Slice meat thinly and arrange on platter lined with salad greens. Mix dressing ingredients together and pour over the beef.

Serves 6

side dishes

chat potatoes

255g/9oz chat potatoes, washed

1 tbsp oil

1 tsp salt

2 tbsps sweet mustard pickles

foil to wrap

1 Choose medium-sized chat potatoes for quick cooking. Place washed potatoes in a bowl and drizzle over the oil and salt, stirring to coat. Wrap each potato in a piece of foil. Place on the barbecue hot plate or grill bars as soon as you light the barbecue and before it is hot enough to cook the meat. This will give the potato a head start. Turn potatoes every few minutes. After barbecue heats and meats are being cooked, turn potatoes more frequently. Test with a skewer if soft, remove and set aside. Potatoes will take about 15-20 minutes according to size and degree of heat.

2 Unwrap potatoes, leaving foil at potato base. Cut a cross in the top and squeeze the base to open out. Spoon mustard pickle in centre and serve immediately.

Serves 4

$^1/_2$ bunch shallots, trimmed and cut into 2cm/$^3/_4$ in lengths

1 medium carrot, thinly sliced

145g/5oz cauliflower florets

115g/4oz snowpeas (mangetout), trimmed

1 small sweet potato, thinly sliced

$^1/_2$ Chinese cabbage, roughly chopped

255mL/9oz teriyaki marinade (page 45)

barbecue

vegetable toss

1 Heat the barbecue hotplate to medium high and oil well. Prepare vegetables and mix together. Pile onto the barbecue and spread out using tongs.

2 Place the cup of marinade in a metal container to heat through, which will make it flow more easily. Toss and cook the vegetables until they soften, then splash over the marinade whilst they complete cooking.

3 Remove to a pre-warmed serving dish while still a little crispy. Serve immediately with barbecued meats.

Note: Other vegetable combinations may be used according to preference.

noodle

and vegetable toss

1 Rinse noodles in hot water and separate. Drain very well. Combine prepared vegetables. Place teriyaki marinade in a small saucepan to heat.

2 Heat the barbecue hotplate to medium-high and oil well. Pile on noodles, toss around a little and add vegetables. Lift and toss with tongs to mix through, then begin splashing on the heated marinade. When well mixed and heated through, remove to a hot serving plate. Serve immediately.

425g/15oz Hokkein noodles

1 large carrot, coarsely grated

2 zucchini (courgette), grated

6 shallots, chopped into 2½cm/ in pieces

1 cup/250mL/8fl oz teriyaki marinade (page 45)

pesto

potato wedges

4 medium-sized potatoes

1 tsp crushed garlic

2 tbsps basil pesto

1 tbsp olive oil

1 tbsp water

55g/2oz grated Parmesan cheese

1 Peel and halve the potatoes, then cut each half into 4-6 wedges. Rinse well and drain then place in a large bowl. Mix garlic, basil pesto, olive oil and water together. Pour over potatoes and toss to coat well. Place in a large foil dish in a single layer if possible and pour over any basil oil mixture remaining in the bowl.

2 Cook over indirect heat in covered barbecue for 40 minutes, turning after 20 minutes. For flattop barbecue, cover with a sheet of foil and place foil tray on the hotplate. Cook 20 minutes then turn and cook 20 minutes more until tender.

3 When cooked, remove to a plate and sprinkle with Parmesan cheese.

pesto tomatoes

12 small even sized tomatoes

2 tbsps basil pesto

2 tbsps grated Romano or Parmesan cheese

I Slice across top of tomato, leaving flap attached. Mix the basil pesto and grated cheese together, lift tomato flap and spread onto the cut surface. Replace flap and spread a little on top. Stand in a foil tray and place tray on the barbecue. Cover with lid or hood and cook for 15 minutes. If flattop barbecue is used, cover tomatoes with foil.

ratatouille

2 medium-sized eggplants (aubergine), cut into 1cm/¹/₂in slices
4 zucchinis (courgettes), cut into 1cm/¹/₂in slices
1 large onion, cut in half & sliced
1 green capsicum (pepper), seeded & sliced
300g/10¹/₂oz jar tomato salsa
1 tsp garlic, crushed

1 Prepare vegetables. Oil a large foil tray and spread base with some of the salsa. Layer in the vegetables, spreading salsa between each layer. Cover with more salsa mixed with garlic. Place over indirect heat in kettle of covered barbecue and cook for 30 minutes. For flattop barbecue, cover tray with foil, stand on a cake-rake placed over the grill bars and cook for 30 minutes.

Salad dressings and sauces

Chilli-Strawberry Sauce

1/2 medium onion, chopped
1 tsp freshly crushed garlic
1 tbsp olive oil
115mL/4fl oz tomato sauce
115g/4oz strawberry jam
55mL/2fl oz beer
2 hot chillis, seeded and
finely chopped
1 tbsp barbecue sauce
1 tsp chilli flakes

I In a small saucepan cook onion and garlic until soft. Stir in all other ingredients and bring to high simmer, do not boil/reduce heat. Cook uncovered for about 10 minutes stirring occasionally, until mixture thickens. Keep handy to the barbecue to brush on meat whilst cooking.

Peanut Sauce

2 tblsp crunchy peanut butter
1 onion finely chopped
1/4 tsp chilli flakes
2 tblsp lemon juice
55mL/2fl oz water

I Combine all ingredients in a saucepan and simmer gently until thickened. Handy to keep warm on the side of the barbecue.

Sweet & Sour Sauce

85mL/3fl oz vinegar
1 tblspn soy sauce
4 1/2 tblsp sugar
1 tblsp tomato sauce
2 tblsp Worchestershire sauce
1/2 tsp salt
1 tsp freshly chopped ginger

I Combine all ingredients together and stir over low heat until sauce thickens. If a thicker sauce is desired add a 1/2 teaspoon blended cornstarch.

Marinades

We recommend that you try some of the tasty supermarket brands of marinade, you will find them easy to use, they give fantastic results. If however you wish to make your own, here are a couple of interesting ones to try.

Teriyaki Marinade

115mL/4fl oz soy sauce
2 tbsps brown sugar
1/2 tsp ground ginger
2 tbsps wine vinegar
1 clove garlic, crushed
2 tbsps tomato sauce

Method: Mix all ingredients together.

Soy and Honey Marinade

55mL/2fl oz soy sauce
2 tbsps honey
1 tbsp sherry
2 cloves garlic, crushed
1 tsp grated fresh ginger

Method: Mix all ingredients together.

Honey & Chilli Marinade

55mL/2fl oz red wine
115mL/4fl oz honey
1/4 tsp ground chilli
1 tsp mustard powder

Method: Mix well together.

Tandoori Paste

2 cloves garlic, peeled
2 1/2 cm/1 in peeled fresh ginger chopped
1 tsp salt
2 tsps coriander (cilantro) seeds
2 tbsps lemon juice
2 tbsps vinegar
1 tsp cumin seeds
1/2 tsp chilli powder
1 tsp tumeric
115g/4oz plain yoghurt

Method: Blend all ingredients except the yoghurt in an electric blender to a smooth paste. Stir into the yoghurt.

Honey and Lemon Marinade

115mL/4fl oz olive oil
2 tbsps lemon juice
1 tbsp honey
1 tbsp freshly crushed garlic
2 bay leaves, crushed

Method: Mix all ingredients together.

Herbed Wine Marinade

115mL/4fl oz soy sauce
2 tbsps brown sugar
1/2 tsp ground ginger
2 tbsp wine vinegar
1 clove garlic, crushed
2 tbsps tomato sauce

Method: Mix all ingredients together.

weights and measures

quick converter

(cook's conversions are not exact)

Metric	Imperial
5mm	$^1/_4$in
1cm	$^1/_2$in
2cm	$^3/_4$in
2$^1/_2$cm	1in
5cm	2in
10$^1/_2$cm	4in
15cm	6in
20cm	8in
23cm	9in
25cm	10in
30cm	12in

metric cups and spoons

(cook's conversions are not exact)

Metric	Cups	Imperial
63mL	$^1/_4$ cup	2$^1/_4$fl oz
85mL	$^1/_3$ cup	3 floz
125mL	$^1/_2$ cup	4$^1/_2$fl oz
250mL	1 cup	8$^3/_4$fl oz
Metric	**Spoons**	
1$^1/_4$mL	$^1/_4$ teaspoon	
2$^1/_2$mL	$^1/_2$ teaspoon	
5mL	1 teaspoon	
20mL	1 tablespoon	

measuring liquids

(cook's conversions are not exact)

Metric	Imperial	
30mL	1fl oz	
55mL	2fl oz	
85mL	3fl oz	
115mL	4fl oz	
125mL	4$^1/_2$fl oz	($^1/_2$ cup)
150mL	5$^1/_4$fl oz	
170mL	6fl oz	
185mL	6$^1/_2$fl oz	
200mL	7fl oz	
225mL	8fl oz	
250mL	8$^3/_4$fl oz	(1 cup)
285mL	10fl oz	
370mL	13fl oz	
400mL	14fl oz	
500mL	17$^1/_2$fl oz	(2 cups)
570mL	20fl oz	(1 pint)
1 litre	35$^1/_3$fl oz	(4 cups)

oven temperatures

°C	°F	Gas Mark
120	250	$^1/_4$
140	275	1
150	300	2
160	325	3
180	350	4
190	375	5
200	400	6
220	425	7
240	475	8
250	500	9

measuring dry ingredients

(cook's conversions are not exact)

Metric	Imperial
15g	$^1/_2$oz
20g	$^2/_3$oz
30g	1oz
55g	2oz
85g	3oz
115g	4oz ($^1/_4$lb)
125g	$4^1/_2$oz
140g	5oz
170g	6oz
200g	7oz
225g	8oz ($^1/_2$lb)
255g	9oz
315g	11oz
370g	13oz
400g	14oz
425g	15oz
455g	16oz (1 lb)
500g	$17^1/_2$oz
680g	$1^1/_2$lb
1kg	2lb 3oz
$1^1/_2$kg	3lb 5oz

Disclaimer: The nutritional information listed under each recipe does not include the nutrient content of garnishes or any accompaniments not listed in specific quantities in the ingredient list. The nutritional information for each recipe is an estimate only, and may vary depending on the brand of ingredients used, and the natural biological variations in the composition of natural foods such as meat, fish, fruit and vegetables. The nutritional information was calculated by using Foodworks dietary analysis software (Version 3, Xyris Software Pty Ltd, Highgate Hill, Queensland, Australia) based on the Australian food composition tables and food manufacturers' data. Where not specified, ingredients are always analysed as average or medium; not small or large.

index

Barbecued toasts 18

Barbecue vegetable toss 39

Barbecued leg of lamb in paper 27

Capsicum barbecued
whole snapper 26

Chargrilled chicken with
mango salsa 23

Chat potatoes 38

Chicken patties with
chilli yoghurt sauce 12

Coriander swordfish steaks 25

Garlic lobster tails
with exotic salad 30

Glazed pork spare ribs 21

Glazed scotch fillet roast with
tomato potato wedges 33

Greek shish kebabs 9

Hot dogs with mustard relish 7

Hot herbed beef salad 36

Lamb fillets with salsa pilaf 28

Main meals **19**

Marinades **45**

Marinated bolar beef with
apple and chilli stuffing 34

Mexican sausages 31

Mustard and honey chicken
drumsticks 17

Noodle and vegetable toss 40

Perfect t-bone steak 10

Pesto potato wedges 41

Pesto tomatoes 42

Piquant pork fillets with polenta 20

Quick meals **5**

Quick ratatouille 43

Quick sausage sizzle 15

Quick sesame chicken wings 14

Salad dressings and sauces 44

Seared tuna with roasted plum
tomatoes 35

Side dishes **37**

Teriyaki prawns 6

Toasted steak sandwiches 11